ARTS AND CRAFTS ACROSS THE KINDERGARTEN
CONTENTS

Language Arts Activities

Math Activities

Science Activities

Social Studies Activities

Contents
Arts and Crafts Across the Curriculum K, SV 1419023535

INTRODUCTION

Arts and Crafts Across the Curriculum is designed to provide arts and crafts activities that correlate with learning standards in the areas of language arts, math, science, and social studies. A wide variety of activities is presented throughout the book. Included are paintings, drawings, puppets, masks, mobiles, headbands, and much more. Regardless of the type of activity used, always allow for and encourage students' creativity.

Preparation for arts and crafts activities is made easier when the basic materials are easily accessible. Make materials such as glue, scissors, markers, crayons, and construction paper available for students to use. Allow plenty of time before doing an activity to collect materials such as paper plates, lunch sacks, or clothespins. Ask parents to help in the collection of recyclables such as paper towel tubes, tissue boxes, cereal boxes, lids, or empty water bottles.

Organization and Features

Each activity consists of two pages. The first page of each activity in the book includes the following:

- a specific standard in one of the core areas of learning which include language arts, math, science, or social studies
- several vocabulary words that students may become familiar with in relation to the topic of the activity
- background information that is related to the topic of the activity that can be discussed with students
- a drawing of the finished product to use as a reference

The second page of each activity includes the following:

- a list of materials needed to complete each activity
- step by step directions for teacher preparation
- step by step directions for the students to do in order to complete the activity
- several questions that the teacher can ask the students about the background information (may also be found on the first page)

In addition, the book contains

- reproducible patterns that are needed for specified activities
- a list of the learning standards referred to throughout the book
- an alphabetical index of the activities that are included in the book

2

Arts and Crafts Across the Curriculum K, SV 1419023535

KINDERGARTEN STANDARDS

Language Arts

- Writes the letters of the alphabet (pages 4–5)
- Recognizes rhyming words (pages 6–7)
- Knows the alphabetical order of letters (pages 8–9)
- Understands the meaning of opposites (pages 10–11)
- Identifies beginning sounds (pages 12–13)
- Retells or acts out the order of important events in stories (pages 14–15)
- Writes labels for artwork (pages 16–17)
- Distinguishes fiction from nonfiction (pages 18–19)

Math

- Constructs graphs using real objects (pages 20–21)
- Knows that ordinal numbers show position (pages 22–23)
- Knows the value of a penny, nickel, dime, and quarter (pages 24–25)
- Associates numerals with sets of objects (pages 26–27)
- Creates and extends a pattern (pages 28–29)
- Tells time by the hour (pages 30–31)
- Measures length using nonstandard units (pages 32–33)
- Identifies circles, triangles, and rectangles including squares (pages 34–35)

Science

- Describes the parts of a plant (pages 36–37)
- Describes characteristics of organisms (pages 38–39)
- Asks questions about organisms (pages 40–41)
- Observes and describes changes in position (pages 42–43)
- Observes characteristics of organisms (pages 44–45)
- Identifies characteristics of organisms such as spiders (pages 46–47)
- Observes and describes properties of rocks (pages 48–49)
- Observes the seasons of the year (pages 50–51)
- Identifies basic needs of living organisms (pages 52–53)
- Identifies and uses senses as tools of observation (pages 54–55)
- Identifies healthy and unhealthy food choices (pages 56–57)
- Studies habitat, structure, and behavior of animals (pages 58–59)

Social Studies

- Identifies land masses and large bodies of water on maps and globes (pages 60–61)
- Identifies customs and traditions (pages 62–63)
- Identifies the contributions of historical figures that helped to shape our nation (pages 64–65)
- Compares life in the past to life in the present (pages 66–67)
- Identifies the flag as a national symbol (pages 68–69)
- Identifies jobs in the community (pages 70–71)
- Understands how basic human needs of food can be met (pages 72–73)
- Identifies likenesses and differences among families (pages 74–75)
- Compares family customs and traditions (pages 76–77)
- Identifies customs associated with national patriotic holidays (pages 78–79)
- Identifies family customs and traditions and explains their importance (pages 80–81)
- Understands the importance of jobs (pages 82–83)

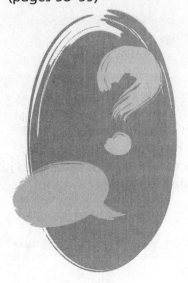

Kindergarten Standards
Arts and Crafts Across the Curriculum K, SV 1419023535

LETTER APPLE TREE

Language Arts Standard
Writes the letters of the alphabet

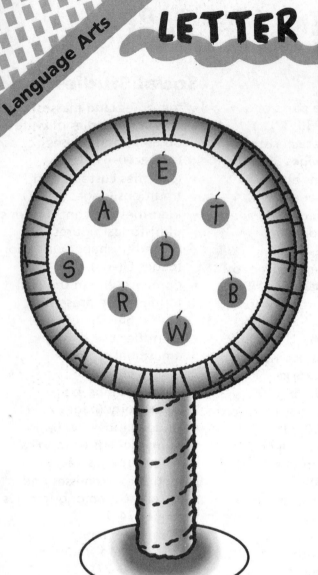

Vocabulary

apples
core
stem
seeds
meat
skin

Discussion

- *Apple* and *alphabet* begin with the letter /a/.
- Apples are attached to the tree by the stem.
- Apples have five seeds that are inside the core.
- The meat of an apple is protected by the skin.
- An apple cut in half across its core will have a symmetrical star shape.
- Apples can be red, yellow, or green in color.

Language Arts Activities
Arts and Crafts Across the Curriculum K, SV 1419023535

Materials

- two six-inch paper plates per student
- one empty bathroom tissue roll per student
- yogurt lids
- red dot stickers
- brown construction paper
- green and brown paint
- paintbrushes
- markers

- scissors
- stapler
- glue

Directions

Teacher Preparation

1. Cut the brown construction paper into quarters.
2. When students have completed their tree, help them staple the pieces together by first pressing one end of the tissue roll flat but leaving the remaining part of the roll round.
3. Staple one paper plate to the flattened end of the tissue roll making sure the painted side faces out.
4. Repeat the procedure by matching the second paper plate to the first one and stapling it on the other side of the tissue roll.
5. Staple both plates together around the remaining edges.

Student Directions

1. Paint the tissue roll brown and let it dry.
2. Paint the bottom side of both paper plates green and let them dry.
3. Write one letter of the alphabet on each red sticker dot.
4. Stick the dots in a pleasing arrangement on both painted plates.
5. Trace the yogurt lid on brown construction paper and cut it out. Younger children may need help tracing the lid.
6. After your teacher has stapled the plates to the tissue roll to form the apple tree, glue the circle to the round end of the roll so that it will stand.

Questions

1. How many letters are in the alphabet? (twenty-six)
2. How many seeds does an apple have? (five)
3. Name the parts of an apple. (stem, skin, meat, core)
4. What color is your favorite apple? (red, yellow, or green)

5

www.harcourtschoolsupply.com
Language Arts Activities
Arts and Crafts Across the Curriculum K, SV 1419023535

HUMPTY DUMPTY RHYME

Vocabulary

cannon
castle
king
soldiers
rhyme

HUMPTY DUMPTY

Humpty Dumpty sat on a wall.
Humpty Dumpty had a great fall.
All the king's horses and all the king's men
Couldn't put Humpty together again!

Discussion

- Many of the familiar nursery rhymes of today originated centuries ago as poems or songs and often made political statements.
- Throughout the years, many of the rhymes were taught for infant amusement.
- During the English Civil War (1642–1649), the Parliamentarians, nicknamed the "Roundheads," fought against the Royalists who supported King Charles.
- The town of Colchester included a castle and was surrounded by a wall. A cannon called Humpty Dumpty was placed on the wall for protection.
- In July of 1648, the wall was damaged and caused the cannon to tumble to the ground.
- All the king's horses (cavalry) and all the king's men (infantry) attempted to raise the cannon to another section of the wall, but it was too heavy, and they did not succeed.

Materials

- one empty cereal box per student
- one paper plate per student
- yogurt lids
- black construction paper
- yellow construction paper
- red paint
- buttons
- paintbrushes
- markers
- masking tape
- scissors
- glue

Directions

Teacher Preparation

1. Tape the open end of the cereal box closed.
2. Cut the black construction paper into one-by-nine-inch strips. Provide each student with four strips.

Student Directions

1. Paint the front side of the cereal box red. Allow it to dry.
2. Use a black marker to draw rectangles on the painted side to resemble the bricks in a wall.
3. Turn the paper plate over with the bottom side up. Then draw eyes, nose, and a mouth on the top half to resemble Humpty Dumpty's face.
4. Color the bottom half of the plate to resemble his pants.
5. Glue two buttons on his pants.
6. Fold four strips of black paper in accordion pleats.
7. Glue one strip on each side of his face for arms and glue two strips at the bottom of the plate for legs.
8. Use a yogurt lid as a template and trace four circles on the yellow paper. Cut them out.
9. Write the four words in the poem that rhyme on the yellow circles.
10. Glue the circles on the black strips as gloves and shoes.
11. Turn the cereal box on its side. Glue Humpty Dumpty on the box as though he is sitting on the "wall."

Questions

1. What word rhymes with wall in the Humpty Dumpty poem? (fall)
2. What are two other words that rhyme in the poem? (men, again)
3. Name three other words that rhyme with *wall* and *fall*. (*ball, call, hall, mall, small, tall*)
4. Who tried to help Humpty Dumpty? (the king's men, soldiers)

7

ALPHABET BLOCKS

Language Arts Standard
Knows the alphabetical
order of letters

THE ALPHABET SONG

A, B, C, D, E, F, G,
H, I, J, K, L, M, N, O, P,
Q, R, S,
T, U, V,
W, X,
Y, and Z.
Now I've said my ABC's.
Next time won't you sing
with me.

Vocabulary

alphabet
letters
sequence
consonants
vowels

Discussion

- There are twenty-six letters in the alphabet.
- Each letter can be written with a capital letter and a lowercase letter.
- Some letters are consonants and some are vowels.
- The letters of the alphabet are arranged in a certain sequence or order.
- The first letter of the alphabet is *Aa* and the last letter is *Zz*.

Language Arts Activities
Arts and Crafts Across the Curriculum K, SV 1419023535

Materials

- patterns on page 84
- one empty cube-shaped tissue box per child
- white spray paint or tempera paint
- construction paper
- sentence strips
- markers
- scissors
- glue
- paintbrushes

Directions

Teacher Preparation

1. Paint tissue boxes with white tempera paint or spray paint. Allow them to dry.
2. Duplicate the letter patterns for each child.
3. Cut twenty-six 1½-by-2-inch pieces of construction paper for each child.
4. Write the alphabet on the sentence strips for each child. To make the strip long enough for all of the letters, glue half of a second strip to the first one.

Student Directions

1. Color a border with markers on each side of the tissue box.
2. Color and cut out the letters *A*, *B*, *C*, and *D*.
3. Glue one letter on each side of the tissue box so that it resembles a toy block.
4. Write a letter of the alphabet on each of the 26 construction paper pieces. Place them in the box.
5. Lay the alphabet strip next to the "block."
6. Reach into the box and pull out one letter.
7. Lay the letter card on the matching letter on the alphabet strip.
8. Repeat the procedure until all of the letters of the alphabet are in order.
9. Point to each letter as you sing "The Alphabet Song."

Questions

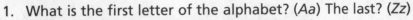

1. What is the first letter of the alphabet? (*Aa*) The last? (*Zz*)
2. What letter comes after the letter *Gg*? (*Hh*)
3. What letter comes before the letter *Tt*? (*Ss*)
4. What is the fourth letter of the alphabet? (*Dd*)
5. What is the next to the last letter of the alphabet? (*Yy*)

Language Arts Activities
Arts and Crafts Across the Curriculum K, SV 1419023535

OPPOSITES IN A FISHBOWL

Language Arts Standard
Understands the meaning of opposites

Vocabulary

opposites
fish
seaweed
rough
smooth

Discussion

- Some plants like seaweed live in water.
- Some fish live in salty ocean water. Some fish live in fresh water.
- Opposites are words whose meanings are completely different from one another.
- There can be opposite sizes like big and little or short and tall.
- There can be opposite textures like rough and smooth.

Language Arts Activities
Arts and Crafts Across the Curriculum K, SV 1419023535

Materials

- patterns on page 86
- one paper plate per student
- blue plastic wrap
- aquarium rocks
- masking tape
- markers
- scissors
- glue

Directions

Teacher Preparation

1. Duplicate the fish patterns for each student.
2. When students have completed their fishbowls, help them cover the plates with plastic wrap and tape the edges to the back of the plate.

Student Directions

1. Glue some aquarium rocks across the bottom of the plate.
2. Draw some tall seaweed and some short seaweed with a green marker.
3. Color and cut out the fish.
4. Write the words *big* and *little* on the appropriate fish.
5. Glue the fish on the plate.
6. With adult help, cover the plate with plastic wrap so that it resembles a fishbowl.

Questions

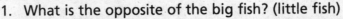

1. What is the opposite of the big fish? (little fish)
2. What is the opposite of the short seaweed? (tall seaweed)
3. Name two kinds of rocks found in a fishbowl that are opposites. (rough, smooth)
4. What makes ocean water the opposite of fresh water? (salt)
5. Water makes things wet. What is the opposite of wet? (dry)

www.harcourtschoolsupply.com
© Harcourt Achieve Inc. All rights reserved.

Language Arts Activities
Arts and Crafts Across the Curriculum K, SV 1419023535

PHONICS AND FLOWERS

Language Arts Standard
Identifies beginning sounds

Vocabulary

ax
elephant
igloo
octopus
umbrella

Discussion

- The vowels /a/, /e/, /i/, /o/, and /u/ make a long and a short sound.
- An ax is a tool used to chop wood.
- An elephant is a very large mammal characterized by a long trunk and long tusks.
- Eskimos make dome-shaped dwellings called igloos that are made from blocks of hard snow.
- An octopus is a sea animal that has a soft, rounded body and eight sucker-bearing tentacles.
- An umbrella is used for protection against the rain and sometimes the sun.

Language Arts Activities
Arts and Crafts Across the Curriculum K, SV 1419023535

Materials

- one shoe box per student
- jumbo craft sticks
- paper muffin cup liners
- plastic milk jug lid
- green and white construction paper
- markers
- scissors
- glue

Directions

Teacher Preparation

1. Use a milk jug lid to trace five circles on the white paper for each student.
2. Cut green paper the size of shoe box lid.
3. When students have glued the green paper on the shoe box lid, cut five slits in it that are the size of the craft sticks.

Student Directions

1. Glue the green paper on the top of the shoe box lid.
2. Write a vowel below each slit on the lid.
3. Cut out five circles.
4. Draw a picture of an ax, an elephant, an igloo, an octopus, and an umbrella on the circles.
5. Glue each picture in the bottom of a muffin liner.
6. Glue each muffin liner on the end of a craft stick to make five flowers.
7. Cut out leaves for each flower from green paper.
8. Glue one or two leaves on each craft stick flower.
9. Insert each flower in the slit whose letter makes the correct beginning sound.

Questions

1. Name the five short vowel sounds. (/a/, /e/, /i/, /o/, and /u/)
2. What is a fruit and begins with the short vowel /a/? (apple)
3. Are the beginning sounds of the words *elf* and *egg* the same or different? (same)
4. What is another word that means sick and begins with the short vowel /i/? (ill)
5. What is a very large bird whose name begins with the short vowel /o/? (ostrich)

Language Arts Activities
Arts and Crafts Across the Curriculum K, SV 1419023535

LITTLE RED HEN STORY MASKS

Language Arts Standard
Retells or acts out the order of important events in stories

Vocabulary

hen

wheat

flour

mill

cooperation

Discussion

- *The Little Red Hen* is a fable which is a story that teaches a moral or lesson.
- Authors often retell or write different versions of popular fables using a special twist that adds interest.
- While the plot of *The Little Red Hen* stays the same, the lazy animal characters may change.
- Compare the characters in two versions of *The Little Red Hen*.
- The grains from a wheat plant are crushed and ground to make flour. The flour is a necessary ingredient for baking bread or cakes.

Language Arts Activities
Arts and Crafts Across the Curriculum K, SV 1419023535

Materials

- patterns on page 85
- paper plates
- red craft feathers
- construction paper
- elastic cord
- pony beads
- hole punch

- stapler
- watercolor paints
- masking tape

- paintbrushes
- glue
- scissors

Directions

Teacher Preparation

1. Enlarge the mask pattern to the size of the paper plate. Cut it out to use as a template. Trace the template on the paper plate.
2. Duplicate the beak pattern.
3. Cut out the mask, the eye holes, and the beak.
4. Staple the beak to the nose section of the mask.
5. Punch a hole on each side of the mask.
6. Thread each end of the elastic cord through a punched hole in the mask and through one bead. Tie a knot to secure. The bead will prevent the elastic from tearing the paper plate when the child puts on the mask.

Student Directions

1. Paint the beak yellow.
2. Paint the mask red.
3. Turn the mask over and tape some red feathers to the top of the mask.
4. Use the mask to retell the story *The Little Red Hen*.

Duck: Follow the same procedure for making the mask except paint the mask yellow, the beak orange, and add yellow feathers.

Dog, Cat, Mouse: Follow the same procedure for making the mask except do not add the beak or feathers. Duplicate on construction paper the appropriate ear pattern on page 85. Have students cut them out and glue them to the mask and use watercolors to decorate it. Then paint the student's nose with black watercolors.

Questions

1. Who was the main character in the story? (the hen)
2. Why did she take the wheat to the mill? (to have it made into flour)
3. What did the other animals say when the hen asked them to help? ("Not I.")
4. What did the hen make from the flour? (bread, cake)
5. Describe what the animals might have done to cooperate with the hen. (help her plant the seeds, take the seeds to the mill, and bake the bread or cake)

15

COLORFUL OCTOPUS

red yellow blue green orange

Vocabulary

octopus
tentacles
suction cups
primary colors
secondary colors

Discussion

- Octopuses (or octopi) have eight tentacles that have suction cups on each one.
- They use the suction cups on the tentacles to grab their prey of all kinds of shellfish. They have a beak inside their mouth opening that is used to crack the shells of their prey.
- Octopuses can change colors to hide from their enemies or when they are happy or angry.
- They do not like to fight but use an inky liquid to confuse their enemy and swim away.
- Primary colors are red, yellow, and blue and are the basis for all other colors.
- Secondary colors are purple, orange, and green. They are made by mixing two primary colors together.

Materials

- one paper bowl per student
- red, yellow, blue, green, orange, purple, black, brown tissue paper
- green paint
- paintbrushes
- white paper
- pencil
- yarn
- craft sticks
- markers
- scissors
- glue

Directions

Teacher Preparation

1. Poke a hole in the center of the bowl.
2. Insert one end of a twelve inch piece of yarn into the hole. Tie a knot on the end that is inside the bowl.
3. Tie the other end of the yarn to a craft stick for a handle.
4. On the inside of the bowl, make eight dots evenly spaced around the edge to indicate where to glue the tentacles.
5. Cut tissue paper into one-by-ten-inch strips. Provide each student with one of each of the eight colors.
6. Cut the white paper into one-by-three-inch pieces. Provide each student with eight pieces.

Student Directions

1. Paint the outside of the bowl green and allow it to dry.
2. Turn the bowl upside down and draw eyes and a mouth on the side.
3. On the inside of the bowl, squeeze a dot of glue on each dot.
4. Glue eight tissue paper strips, one of each color, on the dots.
5. Write each of the eight color words on a piece of white paper.
6. Glue the color word labels on the corresponding tissue paper strips.
7. Hold the octopus by the craft stick and shake gently to make it move.

Questions

1. How many tentacles does an octopus have? (eight)
2. What do octopuses like to eat? (crabs, clams, lobsters; all kinds of shellfish)
3. What two ways can an octopus escape from an enemy? (change colors or squirt an inky liquid)
4. Name the three primary colors. (red, yellow, blue)
5. How is a secondary color made? (by mixing two primary colors)

17

LITTLE PIG SACK PUPPET

Language Arts Standard
Distinguishes fiction
from nonfiction

Vocabulary

pigs
fiction
nonfiction
fact
fantasy

Discussion

- *The Three Little Pigs* is a story about pigs that are characterized as humans.
- The pigs wear clothing like people, talk like people, and use tools to build homes.
- *The Three Little Pigs* is an example of a fiction story, which means it cannot really happen.
- *Pigs are mammals that oink* is a true fact which can be found in a nonfiction book.
- Stories can be fiction with some true facts included such as in *Charlotte's Web* by E. B. White.

Materials

- pattern on page 85
- brown or white lunch sacks
- pink, brown, or black construction paper
- large wiggly eyes
- pink, brown, or black pipe cleaners cut in half
- pencil
- small coffee can lid, potato chip can lid
- crayons or markers
- tape
- scissors
- glue

Directions

Teacher Preparation

Duplicate the pig ear pattern on pink, brown, or black construction paper. Provide two ears per student in the desired color.

Student Directions

1. Trace the coffee can lid for the head and the potato chip lid for the snout on the desired color of construction paper. Cut them out. Draw nostrils with a black marker.
2. Cut out two ears that match the head and snout.
3. Glue the snout and wiggly eyes on the head.
4. Glue the ears to the back of the head and fold them forward.
5. Glue the head on the bottom flap of the sack.
6. Cut out a curved section from the open end of the sack to resemble legs.
7. Cut out a small *V*-section for the hooves. Color the hooves black.
8. Wrap a pipe cleaner around a pencil to form a spiral. Poke one end of the pipe cleaner into the back of the sack for a tail. Tape the pipe cleaner to the inside of the sack to secure it.
9. On the front of the puppet, write or dictate a sentence about a pig that is fantasy.
10. On the back of the puppet, write or dictate a sentence about a pig that is fact.

Questions

1. Is a fiction story fact or fantasy? (fantasy)
2. Is a nonfiction story fact or fantasy? (fact)
3. What kind of story could have a pig riding a bicycle? (fiction)
4. Describe one action in *The Three Little Pigs* story that is fiction. (talks, wears clothes, walks on two feet)
5. Compare the pigs in *The Three Little Pigs* (any version) to the ones in *Pigs* by Gail Gibbons.

19

STUFFED PUMPKIN

Math Standard
Constructs graphs using real objects

Vocabulary

pumpkin
stem
vine
carve
tendril
graph

Discussion

- A pumpkin is a fruit that grows on a leafy vine that lies on the ground.
- Pumpkins are attached to the vine by a stem.
- Sometimes a thin, hairlike tendril is attached to the stem. The tendrils twist around objects on the ground to help anchor the pumpkin and protect it from the wind.
- The inside of a pumpkin has an orangey, yellow pulp; fibrous strands; and seeds.
- Faces can be carved in pumpkins and used at Halloween.
- Graphs can be used to help answer questions.

Questions

1. How does a tendril help the pumpkin? (It twists around things on the ground and helps anchor the pumpkin.)
2. Name the inside parts of a pumpkin. (pulp, strands, and seeds)
3. Which type of face had the most pumpkins on the graph? (Answers will vary.)

Math Activities
Arts and Crafts Across the Curriculum K, SV 1419023535

Materials

- one lunch sack per student
- green and orange paint
- paintbrushes
- newspapers
- green construction paper
- green pipe cleaners
- white plastic shower curtain liner
- pencil
- rubber bands
- blank index cards
- colored plastic tape
- markers
- scissors
- stapler

Directions

Teacher Preparation

1. Make a floor graph by cutting the shower curtain in half. Tape the bottom of one half to the top of the second half to make a long piece of plastic.
2. Use the colored plastic tape to section off three columns on the plastic. Then use the tape to make several rows across the columns. Lay the graph on the floor.
3. When students have stuffed their sacks with newspaper, twist a rubber band around the sack leaving a stem at the top.
4. When students have completed their pumpkins, help them staple the leaf to the stem of the sack.
5. Draw pictures on index cards of a happy, a scary, and a mad jack-o-lantern. Place one picture at the top of each column of the floor graph.

Student Directions

1. Tear newspaper into strips and stuff the sack until it has a round shape.
2. Have an adult twist a rubber band around the sack so that the pumpkin has a stem.
3. Paint the stem green and the pumpkin orange and allow them to dry.
4. Use a black marker to draw a happy, scary, or mad face on the pumpkin.
5. Twist a green pipe cleaner around a pencil to make a tendril.
6. Twist one end of the tendril around the stem.
7. Draw and cut out a large leaf on green construction paper. Have an adult staple it to the stem.
8. Place your pumpkin in the correct column of the floor graph.

Math Activities
Arts and Crafts Across the Curriculum K, SV 1419023535

WATER BOTTLE SNOWMAN

Math Standard
Knows that ordinal numbers show position

Vocabulary

snowman
freeze
crystals
first
second
third

Discussion

- Snow can form in any cloud that is layered.
- If the water droplets in the clouds get too cold and freeze, snowflakes cannot form.
- Snowflakes start as tiny ice crystals that attach to each other. Snowflakes usually have six sides.
- Ordinal numbers are those that show position.
- Ordinal numbers usually come before a noun such as the first child in line or the first day of the month.

Questions

1. Where are snowflakes formed? (in the clouds)
2. Count the six sides of a snowflake using ordinal numbers. (first, second, third, fourth, fifth, sixth)
3. If there were five snowmen in a row, which one is after the second snowman? (the third one)
4. If there were five snowmen in a row, which one is before the fifth snowman? (the fourth one)

Math Activities
Arts and Crafts Across the Curriculum K, SV 1419023535

Materials

- one empty 16-ounce water bottle per student
- one clean 4-ounce snack size yogurt container per student
- white and black tempera paint
- one tennis ball
- scissors

- one or two spools of narrow ribbon
- liquid dishwashing soap

- paintbrushes
- markers
- hot glue gun

Directions

Teacher Preparation

1. Help the students tie a piece of ribbon around the bottle to resemble a scarf.
2. Pour a small amount of white paint into the water bottle and tighten the lid securely.
3. Mix a few drops of dishwashing liquid in the black paint so that it will adhere to the plastic yogurt cup.
4. When students have completed their snowman and have painted the yogurt container black, turn the yogurt container upside down and hot glue it on the top of the bottle for a hat.

Student Directions

1. Shake or roll the bottle until the inside is completely covered with white paint. Shake again when paint settles.
2. Draw black eyes, an orange carrot-shaped nose, and a red mouth with markers on the top part of the bottle.
3. Draw two or three buttons below the face of the snowman.
4. Have an adult help tie a piece of ribbon around the bottle to resemble a scarf.
5. Paint the yogurt container black and allow it to dry.
6. Have an adult hot glue the yogurt container on the snowman as a hat.
7. Place several snowmen in a row on the floor. Stand several feet away and try to knock over a snowman by rolling a tennis ball. Identify which snowman fell over such as the first one, third one, etc.

Math Activities
Arts and Crafts Across the Curriculum K, SV 1419023535

TISSUE BOX PIGGY BANK

Math Standard
Knows the value of a penny,
nickel, dime, and quarter

Vocabulary

money
penny
nickel
dime
quarter

Discussion

- Money is used to buy goods and services.
- A penny is worth one cent.
- A nickel is worth five cents.
- A dime is worth ten cents.
- A quarter is worth twenty-five cents.

Math Activities
Arts and Crafts Across the Curriculum K, SV 1419023535

Materials

- one empty tissue box per student
- two empty bathroom tissue rolls per student
- one six-inch paper plate per student
- pink construction paper
- pink pipe cleaners
- yogurt lid
- pattern on page 85
- pink paint
- paintbrushes
- pencil
- markers
- scissors
- glue

Directions

Teacher Preparation
1. Duplicate two pig ears on pink construction paper for each student.
2. Cut the tissue rolls in half.
3. Glue a tissue roll half to each corner of the bottom of the tissue box for legs.
4. Cut construction paper into quarters.
5. Help students poke a hole in the box for the tail.

Student Directions
1. Paint the top of a paper plate and the tissue box with legs pink. Allow them to dry.
2. Trace the yogurt lid on pink paper for the snout. Cut it out.
3. Glue the snout on the paper plate head.
4. Cut out the two ears and glue them on the head.
5. Draw eyes and nostrils with a black marker.
6. Glue the head to one end of the tissue box.
7. Have an adult help poke a hole in the other end of the box.
8. Twist a pipe cleaner around the pencil to form a spiral. Insert one end through the hole in the box to form a tail.
9. Use the piggy bank to save coins. Name the coins as they are put in the bank.

Questions

1. How many cents is a penny worth? A nickel? A dime? A quarter? (one cent, five cents, ten cents, twenty-five cents)
2. How many cents does one nickel and two pennies make? (seven cents)
3. How much are two nickels worth? (ten cents)
4. Name two other ways to make ten cents. (one nickel and five pennies; ten pennies)
5. How many nickels does it take to make a quarter? (five)

25

www.harcourtschoolsupply.com
Math Activities
Arts and Crafts Across the Curriculum K, SV 1419023535

SQUIRREL IN A TREE

Math Standard
Associates numerals
with sets of objects

Vocabulary

autumn
squirrel
acorns
leaves
tree

Discussion

- The squirrel's diet consists of nuts, seeds, and fruit.
- Squirrels chew on branches of the tree to sharpen and clean their teeth.
- Squirrels do not hibernate but store great quantities of food for the winter.
- A squirrel can use its tail for balancing as it leaps from tree to tree and can also use it as a blanket to wrap around itself in cold weather.
- The eyes of the squirrel are located high on their head so that they can see in front and behind them.

www.harcourtschoolsupply.com

Math Activities
Arts and Crafts Across the Curriculum K, SV 1419023535

Materials

- pattern on page 86
- one paper towel tube per student
- small resealable bags
- acorns or brown beans
- tissue paper in fall colors
- brown paint
- dice
- glue
- crayons

- scissors
- paintbrushes

Directions

Teacher Preparation

1. Duplicate a copy of the squirrel for each student.
2. Cut a generous supply of tissue paper into one-inch squares.
3. Cut a hole in the side of the paper towel tube to resemble a hole in the side of a tree.
4. Make several three-inch cuts on one end of the tube. Bend the sections outward to resemble the branches of a tree.

Student Directions

1. Paint the paper towel tube brown and allow it to dry.
2. Crumple a generous amount of tissue paper squares and glue them on the "branches" of the tree.
3. Color and cut out the squirrel pattern.
4. Insert the squirrel in the tree hole. Glue it in place so that it appears to be in the tree.
5. Count twelve acorns or beans into a resealable bag.
6. Stand the "tree" on a flat surface and roll two dice.
7. Drop the corresponding number of acorns in the tree for the squirrel.
8. Lift the tree to remove the acorns and roll again.

Questions

1. Describe two ways a squirrel uses its tail. (for balance or warmth)
2. What kind of food does a squirrel eat? (nuts, seeds, fruit)
3. If a squirrel found 2 acorns and then found 3 more acorns, how many acorns would he have? (5)
4. A squirrel buried 6 acorns. He ate 3 of them. How many did he have left? (3)
5. A mother squirrel had 3 boy babies and 1 girl baby. How many babies did she have? (4)

27

PATTERNED TUBE SNAKE

Math Standard
Creates and extends a pattern

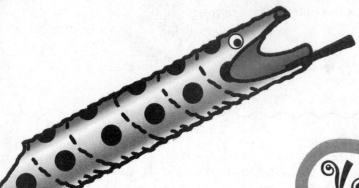

Vocabulary

pattern

snake

scales

reptile

coldblooded

Discussion

- Snakes are reptiles that are coldblooded and rely on the heat of the sun to control their body temperature.
- Their bodies are legless and are covered with scales.
- About two-thirds of all snakes are not poisonous.
- Body patterns differ dramatically among the snake species. Their markings can be spots, horizontal or vertical stripes, diamond shapes, or a combination.
- Snakes use their tongues to taste and smell their environment.
- Snakes do not have moveable eyelids, but their eyes are covered with a transparent scale.

Math Activities
Arts and Crafts Across the Curriculum K, SV 1419023535

Materials

- one paper towel tube per student
- construction paper
- narrow red ribbon
- medium-sized wiggly eyes
- craft items such as rick-rack and ribbon
- dot stickers
- stapler
- markers
- scissors
- glue

Directions

Teacher Preparation

1. Cut various colors of construction paper in pieces that are six-inches-by-eleven-inches.
2. When students have decorated and covered their tube, press one end of the tube flat and cut it to form a point.
3. Cut a curved piece off of both sides on the opposite end of the tube to form a mouth.

Student Directions

1. Decorate a piece of construction paper of desired color with ribbon, rick-rack, dot stickers, or markers. Repeat the pattern across the length of the paper.
2. Attach the decorated paper to the paper towel tube with glue. Have an adult staple the ends of the paper together if necessary to hold in place.
3. Have an adult cut the tube to form the head and the tail.
4. Glue two wiggly eyes on the head.
5. Glue a two-inch piece of red ribbon in the mouth for a tongue.

Questions

1. What is a snake's body covered with? (scales)
2. How many legs does a snake have? (none)
3. Why does a snake flick its tongue in and out? (to taste and smell the air)
4. Are all snakes poisonous? (no)
5. Why don't snakes blink? (They have no moveable eyelids.)

Math Activities
Arts and Crafts Across the Curriculum K, SV 1419023535

HICKORY DICKORY BOX CLOCK

Math Standard
Tells time by the hour

Vocabulary

clock
time
hour
mouse
hands

HICKORY DICKORY DOCK

Hickory Dickory Dock.
The mouse ran up the clock.
The clock struck one
And the mouse ran down.
Hickory Dickory Dock.

Discussion

- The front of a clock that displays the numbers is called the face.
- The hour and minute are measured by the hands of the clock.
- "Hickory Dickory Dock" was thought to have originated in America around 1744 as a way to teach children time.
- Time can be written digitally or can be read according to the placement of the hands on a timepiece.
- The hour is followed by a colon and two zeroes on a digital clock.

Materials

- patterns on page 87
- six-inch paper plates
- one shoe box per student
- one plastic milk jug lid per student
- brown or gray construction paper
- brown craft paper

- tape
- brads
- crayons or markers
- scissors

- glue

Directions

Teacher Preparation

1. Duplicate a clock face and clock hands for each student.
2. Duplicate four mice for each student on brown or gray construction paper.
3. Cover the lid of the shoe box with brown craft paper.
4. Cut a mouse hole at one end of the lid.
5. Help students poke a hole through the paper plate and attach the clock hands with a brad.

Student Directions

1. Color the clock hands.
2. Cut out the clock hands and clock face.
3. Glue the clock face in the center of the paper plate.
4. With an adult's help, use the brad to attach the hand to the clock.
5. Glue the clock to the shoe box lid on the opposite end of the mouse hole.
6. Glue a milk jug lid above the mouse hole. Draw a thick, black line from the clock to the milk jug lid to complete the pendulum.
7. Cut out the four mice.
8. Write a different time such as 1:00 or 8:00 on each mouse.
9. Place the mice inside the shoe box and stand the box so that the clock is upright.
10. Reach inside the mouse hole and pull out one mouse. Read the time and move the hands on the clock to the correct hour. Repeat with all of the mice.

Questions

1. What is the front of a clock or watch called? (the face)
2. Which hand points to the hour on the clock? (the short hand)
3. Which hand points to the minute on the clock? (the long hand)
4. What number does the minute hand point to on each hour? (twelve)
5. What could the mouse do if the clock struck two? (The second verse of the rhyme actually says the mouse said, "Boo.")

Math Activities
Arts and Crafts Across the Curriculum K, SV 1419023535

RAIN CLOUD MOBILE

Math Standard
Measures length using
nonstandard units

Vocabulary

cloud

rain

ruler

measure

inch

Discussion

- A cloud is formed when water drops are heated by the sun and evaporation occurs.
- The drops then hit the cold air in the upper atmosphere and condensation occurs, which causes the drops to fall back to the ground in the form of rain.
- Length can be measured by nonstandard tools such as paper clips, plastic cubes, or blocks.
- A ruler is a straight tool marked off in standard units and is used to measure length.
- The most common ruler in the United States is divided into twelve inches, which equal one foot.

Materials

- one wire hanger per student
- white craft paper
- blue crepe paper streamers
- paper clips
- pencil
- glue
- masking tape
- scissors

Directions

Teacher Preparation

1. Draw two clouds on the white craft paper for each student that are slightly larger than the hanger.
2. Cut five crepe paper streamers of various lengths for each student.
3. Help students tape the hanger to the back of the cloud.

Student Directions

1. Cut out the two clouds.
2. Glue five streamers across the bottom of one cloud.
3. Measure the length of each streamer using the paper clips.
4. Write the length of each streamer on the cloud above the streamer.
5. Have an adult help tape the hanger to the back of the cloud.
6. Glue the second cloud to the back of the first one so that it covers the entire hanger except for the hook.
7. Find a place to hang the cloud mobile.

Questions

1. What is a cloud made of? (water drops)
2. What are the water drops called when they fall from the clouds? (rain)
3. Which tool did you use to measure the paper strips? (paper clip)
4. Which of the strips was the shortest? The longest? (Answers will vary.)
5. Count the inches on a ruler. How many are there? (twelve)

33

Arts and Crafts Across the Curriculum K, SV 1419023535

SHAPELY CLOWN

Math Standard
Identifies circles, triangles, and
rectangles including squares

Vocabulary

circle
triangle
square
rectangle
oval

Discussion

- The study of the shape, size, and position of geometric figures is called geometry.
- Geometry is meaningful and important because the world is full of geometric shapes.
- A circle is a closed curve on a plane with all points of the curve at the same distance from the center.
- A triangle is an enclosed plane figure that has three line segments for sides. The sides meet at three points, and the sum of the three angles is always 180°.
- A rectangle is a symmetrical four-sided plane figure with four right angles.
- A square is a rectangle with four sides of equal length.

Math Activities
Arts and Crafts Across the Curriculum K, SV 1419023535

Math

Materials

- patterns on page 88
- plastic gallon ice cream tub lid
- potato chip canister lid
- construction paper
- one round red balloon per student
- round buttons
- pencil
- markers
- tape

- scissors
- glue

Directions

 Teacher Preparation

1. Cut a two-by-eight-inch rectangle from the desired color of construction paper for each student.
2. Cut several two-inch squares of a desired color for each student.
3. Cut several one-by-six-inch orange rectangles for each student.
4. Duplicate the triangle hat and oval mouth for each student.
5. Help students blow up a balloon to the size of a clown's nose and tie it. Poke a hole through the center of the face and insert the knot of the balloon through to the back. Tape the knot to the paper.

Student Directions

1. Trace the large lid on white construction paper. Cut it out.
2. Trace the small lid on red construction paper. Cut it out.
3. Cut out the large triangle.
4. Glue the small red circle on the top of the triangle and the large rectangle across the bottom to make the hat.
5. Glue the hat on the top of the white circle.
6. Color and cut out the oval mouth. Glue it on the clown face.
7. Use a black marker to draw two large plus signs for the eyes. Glue round buttons on top of the black lines to complete the clown eyes.
8. Glue the orange rectangles on each side of the clown's face for hair.
9. Glue squares around the bottom edge of the clown's face for a collar.
10. Have an adult help blow up a red balloon and attach it to the clown's face for the nose.

Questions

1. What shape is a wheel? (circle)
2. Name something that is shaped like a rectangle. (Answers will vary.)
3. How many sides does a triangle have? (three)
4. How are a square and a rectangle the same? Different? (They both have four sides; the sides of a square are all the same length.)
5. Name two shapes that are closed curves. (circle and oval)

35

Math Activities
Arts and Crafts Across the Curriculum K, SV 1419023535

SUNFLOWER PLANTS

Science Standard
Describes the parts of a plant

Vocabulary

seeds
embryo
stem
leaves
petals
roots

Discussion

- Inside each seed is a new baby plant called an embryo.
- The roots of a plant take in water and food (minerals) from the soil and anchor the plant.
- The stem is made up of little tubes that transport water through the plant.
- Leaves make food for the plant with a green substance called chlorophyll.
- Flowers produce seeds that grow new plants.
- Flower petals with their bright colors and sweet scent help attract insects and birds to help with pollination.

Science Activities
Arts and Crafts Across the Curriculum K, SV 1419023535

Materials

- one paper plate per student
- one empty wrapping paper tube per student
- sunflower seeds
- green construction paper
- white yarn
- paintbrushes
- pencil

- scissors
- green, yellow, and brown tempera paint

- hot glue gun
- glue

Science

Directions

Teacher Preparation

1. Help students trace and cut out two handprints on green construction paper.
2. When students have completed their sunflower, use hot glue to attach the head of the flower to the tube stem.
3. If desired, stand the sunflowers in a small, empty trash can for display.

Student Directions

1. Paint the wrapping paper tube green for the stem and allow it to dry.
2. Paint the center circle of the paper plate brown and the remaining part yellow for the head of the flower. Allow it to dry.
3. Make the petals of the flower by cutting in from the edge of the paper plate up to the brown circle. Repeat cuts every two inches.
4. Spread a layer of glue in the brown center of the paper plate.
5. Press a generous amount of sunflower seeds into the glue.
6. Have an adult use hot glue to attach the sunflower head to the stem.
7. Glue yarn to the bottom of the tube for roots.
8. Have an adult help trace and cut out two handprints for leaves from green construction paper.
9. Glue the handprint leaves on the tube stem.

Questions

1. Name two ways that the roots help a plant. (Roots take in water and food from the soil and anchor the plant.)
2. What part of the plant carries water to the different parts? (the stem)
3. What is inside each seed? (a baby plant, embryo)
4. What do the leaves of a plant do? (make food for the plant)
5. Name the part of the plant that makes new seeds. (the flower)

37

Arts and Crafts Across the Curriculum K, SV 1419023535

STEGOSAURUS HAT

Vocabulary

dinosaurs
extinct
stegosaurus
plant eater
bony plates
spikes

Discussion

- Stegosaurus dinosaurs have been extinct for over 140 million years.
- Stegosauri were plant eaters.
- These dinosaurs grew up to 30 feet long which is about the length of a school bus.
- A stegosaurus had bony plates that extended down its back and had spikes at the end of its tail. These bony plates were thought to have provided protection for the dinosaur.
- They walked on four legs, but their back two legs were twice as long as the front legs.

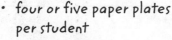

Materials

- four or five paper plates per student
- tempera paints
- paintbrushes
- yarn
- stapler
- hole punch
- scissors

Directions

Teacher Preparation

1. Help students staple the folded paper plates together.
2. Help them staple the folded plates together end-to-end.
3. Punch a hole on the fold of the plate at the end and tie a short piece of yarn through the hole.
4. Punch a hole on two sides of the remaining paper plate. Tie a 12-inch piece of yarn through each hole.
5. Punch a third hole between the two other holes.
6. Tie the loose end of the yarn that is attached to the folded paper plates through the third hole and tie.
7. Place the flat paper plate on top of the student's head and tie the yarn below the chin so that folded plates hang freely down the back.

Student Directions

1. Paint the bottom side of the paper plates using the desired colors. Allow them to dry.
2. Fold all but one of the plates in half.
3. Have an adult help staple the plates together.
4. When all of the plates are stapled and tied together, have an adult help tie the "hat" on.

Questions

1. Were stegosaurus dinosaurs meat-eaters or plant-eaters? (plant-eaters)
2. A stegosaurus was about the same length as what kind of vehicle? (a school bus)
3. Describe the back and tail of the stegosaurus. (It had bony plates on its back and spikes on it tail.)
4. What was unusual about the stegosaurus's legs? (The back legs were longer than the front legs.)
5. What does it mean when we say dinosaurs are extinct? (They are no longer alive.)

Science Activities
Arts and Crafts Across the Curriculum K, SV 1419023535

SCALY FISH

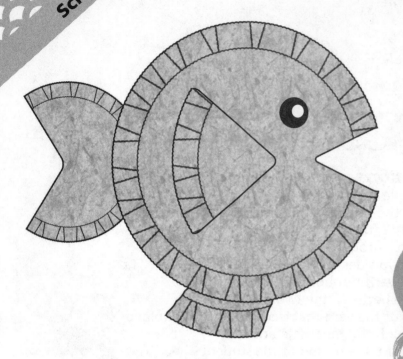

Vocabulary
fish
skeleton
scales
fins
gills

Discussion

- Fish have skeletons that give them their shape.
- Their bodies are covered with bony scales that are waterproof and give them protection.
- Instead of lungs, fish breathe with gills that remove the oxygen from the water.
- Fish have fins, and most fish use their tail fins to move their bodies through the water.
- They use their other fins to help them steer.

Science Activities
Arts and Crafts Across the Curriculum K, SV 1419023535

Materials

- one large paper plate per student
- one small paper plate per student
- large wiggly eyes
- tempera paints
- sponges
- clothespins
- stapler
- scissors
- glue

Directions

Teacher Preparation

1. Cut a quarter section out of the small paper plate. Save for use as a fin.
2. Staple the edge of the small plate to the edge of the large plate so that the cutout resembles a tail fin.
3. Cut out a small section of the large plate opposite the tail fin to look like the mouth of the fish.
4. Staple the section from the mouth to the bottom edge of the large plate for a small fin.
5. Staple the section cut from the small plate to the center of the large plate to look like a side fin.
6. Cut sponges into small pieces and moisten with water.

Student Directions

1. Use a clothespin to grasp a sponge and dip the sponge in the desired color of paint.
2. Cover the fish with sponge prints to resemble the scales on a fish and allow it to dry.
3. Glue a wiggly eye near the mouth of the fish.

Questions

1. What gives a fish its shape? (skeleton)
2. What is a fish's body covered with? (scales)
3. Tell what a fish uses to breathe with. (gills)
4. How does a fish move through the water? (moves the tail fin)
5. What would you like to know about a fish? (Answers will vary.)

4·1

STUFFED SUN

Science Standard
Observes and describes
changes in position

Vocabulary

sun
star
Earth
rotates
revolves

Discussion

- The sun is a star which is a burning ball of gas.
- The sun is the closest star to Earth and provides it with heat and light.
- Earth revolves around the sun and at the same time rotates on its axis.
- The sun seems to change position in the sky because Earth is continually rotating.
- The sun can only shine on half of Earth at a time. One half of Earth experiences daytime while the other half experiences nighttime.

Science Activities
Arts and Crafts Across the Curriculum K, SV 1419023535

Materials

- two paper plates per student
- yellow and orange construction paper
- yellow, orange, and red tempera paint
- plastic wrap with bubbles
- clean meat trays
- sponges
- markers
- scissors
- glue

Directions

Teacher Preparation

1. Cut a generous supply of one-by-nine-inch strips of yellow and orange construction paper.
2. Place a sponge in a meat tray and pour some paint over the sponge. Make a tray for each color of paint.
3. Cut the plastic wrap into two-inch squares.

Student Directions

1. Glue orange and yellow paper strips around the edge of one plate for the sun's rays. Turn the circle over to paint.
2. Press the plastic wrap on the sponge to get some paint.
3. Press the painted plastic wrap on both plates to make the burning gases.
4. Repeat the process with all three colors to cover the sun. Allow the paint to dry.
5. Draw a happy face on one side of the sun.
6. Glue the two plates together using only a line of glue around the edge. Younger students may need help gluing the plates together.

Questions

1. Name the star closest to Earth. (the sun)
2. Why does the sun change positions in the sky? (because Earth is always turning)
3. Why does the sun seem to change its position in the sky? (Earth is rotating.)
4. Name an activity you might do when the sun appears in the morning sky. (get out of bed, get dressed, eat breakfast, go to school)
5. Look at the position of the sun three different times during the day. Describe what you were doing at each time. (Answers will vary.)

43

WINDSOCK BUTTERFLY

Science Standard
Observes characteristics of organisms

Vocabulary

butterfly
head
thorax
abdomen
insect

Discussion

- Butterflies are flying insects with large, scaly wings.
- They have two pairs of wings that are covered with colorful, iridescent scales that are in overlapping rows.
- They have three body parts which include a head, thorax, and abdomen.
- Butterflies have six jointed legs that are attached to the thorax. They also have a pair of antennae and an exoskeleton or protective shell.
- Adult butterflies eat only liquids like flower nectar through a strawlike mouth called a proboscis.

Science Activities
Arts and Crafts Across the Curriculum K, SV 1419023535

Materials

- patterns on page 89
- one lunch sack per student
- crepe paper streamers
- white construction paper
- hole punch
- yarn
- markers
- scissors
- glue

Directions

Teacher Preparation

1. Duplicate two wings and a body on white construction paper for each student.
2. Cut off the bottom end of the lunch sacks.
3. Help students punch holes on both sides of the sack at the top end and tie a piece of yarn through each hole.

Student Directions

1. Cut several crepe paper streamers to the desired length.
2. Glue the streamers around the inside edge of one end of the sack.
3. Color and cut out the wings and the body patterns. Glue the wings to the body.
4. Glue the butterfly to one side of the lunch sack, positioning it so that the streamers are at the bottom end of the body.
5. Have an adult help punch holes on both sides of the sack at the top end and then tie a piece of yarn through each hole.
6. Take the windsock outside and hold it high to let the wind blow through it.

Questions

1. How many legs does a butterfly have? (six)
2. Name the three parts of a butterfly's body. (head, thorax, abdomen)
3. What part of the body are the legs attached to? (thorax)
4. What are the butterfly's wings covered with? (scales)
5. What do adult butterflies eat? (flower nectar)

SPECTACULAR SPIDER HATS

Science Standard
Identifies characteristics of organisms such as spiders

Vocabulary

arachnids
cephalothorax
abdomen
silk
spinnerets

Discussion

- Spiders are arachnids that have eight legs and are not insects that have six legs.
- They have two major body parts, the cephalothorax (the head and chest) and the abdomen.
- A spider's legs are jointed and are attached to the cephalothorax.
- Most spiders have eight eyes. Web building spiders have poor eyesight while hunting spiders have excellent eyesight for short distances.
- Spiders have silk spinning glands at the tip of their abdomen called spinnerets.
- Spiders use silk to build webs, catch their prey, and make egg sacs.

Science Activities
Arts and Crafts Across the Curriculum K, SV 1419023535

Materials

- black and green construction paper
- sentence strips
- white crepe paper streamers
- green dot stickers

- hole punch
- markers
- scissors

- glue

Directions

Teacher Preparation

1. Cut one-by-nine-inch strips from the black construction paper. Provide each student with eight strips.
2. Draw four small *X*'s on each side of the center of a sentence strip to indicate where legs will be attached. Space the marks so that the legs will be above students' ears.
3. Punch a generous supply of small dots from green construction paper.
4. Cut crepe paper streamers in two-foot lengths.
5. Adjust the sentence strip to fit students' heads and staple it to form a headband hat.

Student Directions

1. Fold eight black strips in accordion pleats for legs.
2. Glue legs on the indicated marks on the sentence strip.
3. Place two green dot stickers in the center of the sentence strip for large eyes.
4. Glue six small green dots around the large dots for the remaining eyes.
5. Have an adult adjust the sentence strip to fit and staple it to form the headband.
6. Glue two or three pieces of crepe paper to the back of the headband to resemble silk threads.

Questions

1. How do a spider's legs differ from an insect's legs? (A spider has eight legs and an insect has six.)
2. Name the two parts of a spider's body. (cephalothorax and abdomen)
3. What part of the spider's body are the legs attached to? (cephalothorax)
4. How many eyes do most spiders have? (eight)
5. What is a spinneret? (the part of a spider's body that makes the silk threads)

Science Activities
Arts and Crafts Across the Curriculum K, SV 1419023535

ROCK RINGS

Science Standard
Observes and describes
properties of rocks

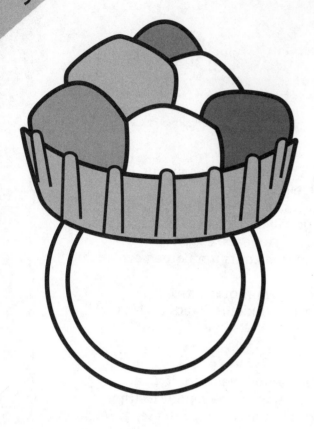

Vocabulary

minerals

lava

igneous

sedimentary

metamorphic

Discussion

- Rocks are made up of one or more minerals that vary in color and texture.
- Rocks are classified according to how they are formed.
- Igneous rocks are formed from the lava of a volcano.
- Sedimentary rocks are formed by layers of sediments from sand, mud, animal material, or plant material.
- Seventy percent of all rocks on Earth's surface are sedimentary.
- Metamorphic rocks are formed by adding heat and pressure to igneous or sedimentary rocks.

Science Activities
Arts and Crafts Across the Curriculum K, SV 1419023535

Materials

- one metal bottle cap per student (not twist caps)
- multicolored aquarium rocks
- awl (small pointed tool for making holes in bottle caps)
- glue
- hammer
- twist-ties

Directions

Teacher Preparation

1. Use the hammer and awl to make two holes in each bottle cap.
2. Insert the two ends of the twist-tie through the holes on the top side of the cap. Leave a finger-sized loop on the top. Turn the cap over and twist the ends together to secure the loop.

Student Directions

1. Fill the bottle cap with a layer of glue.
2. Cover the glue with aquarium rocks.
3. Add another layer of glue and more rocks.
4. Repeat the procedure, if desired.
5. Allow the glue to dry and wear the ring.

Questions

1. What are rocks made of? (minerals)
2. How are igneous rocks made? (lava from a volcano cools)
3. Rocks formed by layers of sand or mud are what kind of rocks? (sedimentary)
4. Heat and pressure can change igneous and sedimentary rocks into what kind of rocks? (metamorphic)
5. Most of the rocks on Earth's surface are what kind of rocks? (sedimentary)

SEASONAL TISSUE BOX

Science Standard
Observes the seasons of the year

Vocabulary

seasons

spring

summer

fall

winter

Discussion

- The seasons of the year are determined by the position of Earth in relation to the sun.
- In the spring, the days gradually get longer, the nights get shorter, and the temperatures get warmer. This is the time of the year that many plants bloom and many animals have their babies.
- The days are longer than the nights during the summer, and temperatures are hot.
- In the fall, the days gradually get shorter and the nights get longer. The temperatures also begin to get cooler. Many trees lose their leaves.
- The nights are longer than the days in the winter, and the temperatures get cold enough for snow in many regions.

Science Activities
Arts and Crafts Across the Curriculum K, SV 1419023535

Materials

- pattern on page 90
- one cube-shaped tissue box per student (with tissues if possible)
- red, yellow, orange, and brown tissue paper
- white tempera paint
- white chalk
- pencil
- markers
- scissors
- glue

Directions

Teacher Preparation

1. Duplicate the pattern to make four trees for each student.
2. Cut a generous supply of red, yellow, orange, and brown tissue paper into one-inch squares.

Student Directions

1. Color and cut out four trees.
2. Color the background of each tree blue.
3. Draw snow with chalk for winter on the first trunk.
4. Draw a few green leaves on the second trunk. Dip the eraser end of the pencil in white paint and stamp circles on the tree for the blossoms in spring. When the paint is dry, draw a yellow dot in the center of each blossom.
5. Draw lots of green leaves on the third tree for summer.
6. Twist and glue red, yellow, orange, and brown tissue squares on the fourth tree for fall. Glue a few falling to the ground.
7. Write the name of each season on each picture.
8. Glue each tree on the side of the tissue box in the correct order of the seasons.

Questions

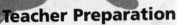

1. How many seasons are there in a year? (four)
2. During which season do many animals have their babies? (spring)
3. When are the temperatures the hottest? (during the summer)
4. During which season are the nights the longest? (winter)
5. In which season do many trees loose their leaves? (fall)

51

TURTLE MAGNET

Science Standard
Identifies basic needs
of living organisms

Vocabulary
reptiles
turtles
tortoises
shell
vertebrate

Discussion

- Reptiles, including turtles and tortoises, are coldblooded vertebrates that breathe air with lungs and are covered with scales. Their backbone is attached to the shell.
- Turtles and tortoises, like most other reptiles, lay eggs that have soft, leathery shells. The nest temperature determines the sex of the turtles. Males need a colder nest and females need a warmer nest.
- Turtles that live in cold climates hibernate during the winter.
- Turtles that live mostly in the water are called terrapins and have shells that are flatter.
- Tortoises live mostly on dry land but can go in the water if necessary.
- Turtles do not have teeth but do have a beak and eat plants, fruits, insects, and even pieces of meat.

Materials

- pattern on page 91
- one wooden clothespin per student
- cardboard egg cartons (one cup per student)
- roll of magnetic tape
- small wiggly eyes
- green construction paper
- green tempera paint
- paintbrushes
- markers
- scissors
- glue

Directions

Teacher Preparation

1. Duplicate the turtle on green construction paper for each student.
2. Cut the egg cartons apart so that each student has a single egg cup. Cut the edges as straight as possible.
3. Cut magnetic tape into two-inch pieces.

Student Directions

1. Paint the outside of the egg cup green.
2. Cut out the turtle body. Younger students may need help cutting.
3. Squeeze a line of glue around the edge of the egg cup and glue it in the center of the turtle for the shell.
4. Glue two wiggly eyes on the head and draw nostrils with a black marker.
5. Stick a strip of magnetic tape on one side of a wooden clothespin.
6. Put some glue on the other side of the clothespin and glue the turtle body on it. Make sure that the head of the turtle faces that end that opens when the clothespin is squeezed.
7. Use the turtle magnet to hold special papers on a magnetic surface such as a refrigerator.

Questions

1. What are reptiles, including turtles, covered with? (scales)
2. How do turtles have their babies? (lay soft, leathery eggs)
3. How do turtles stay warm in the winter? (They hibernate or sleep.)
4. Where do tortoises prefer to live? (on dry land)
5. Do turtles chew with teeth? (No, they have a beak but no teeth.)

53

SCENTED RAINBOWS

Science Standard
Identifies and uses senses
as tools of observation

Vocabulary

senses
sight
smell
hearing
touch
taste

Discussion

- Information is received through the five senses which include seeing, hearing, smelling, tasting, and touching.
- Our eyes work like video cameras and allow us to see.
- Taste buds allow us to experience tastes that are sweet, salty, sour, and bitter.
- Our nose allows us to smell thousands of different odors both pleasant and unpleasant.
- Our nose works together with the taste buds to create flavors of foods.
- The skin is the main organ of the sense of touch. The nerve endings in the skin can detect pressure, pain, and temperature.
- The ear is the organ that provides hearing and allows us to keep our balance.

Science Activities
Arts and Crafts Across the Curriculum K, SV 1419023535

Materials

- white construction paper
- finger paint (colors of the rainbow)
- shaving cream
- tub of water
- hand towels
- glue

Directions

Teacher Preparation

1. Place a small dab of one color of finger paint on the white construction paper. Repeat for each color.
2. Provide a tub of water and a towel for students to wash their hands.
3. When students have completed the rainbow, mix equal amounts of shaving cream and glue together.

Student Directions

1. Use the finger paints to make a rainbow on the white construction paper.
2. Wash your hands after each color.
3. Dip your fingers into the shaving cream mixture and make clouds at each end of the rainbow.
4. Wash your hands again.
5. Name the senses that you used while making the rainbow. (You see and touch the paint, hear your fingers rub against the paper, and smell the shaving cream.)

Questions

1. Which one of the five senses works like a camera? (eyes)
2. Name the four flavors that our mouths can taste. (sweet, salty, sour, and bitter)
3. Which part of the body allows us to hear? (ear)
4. Which two senses work together to create food flavors? (smell and taste)
5. Name the five senses. (sight, smell, touch, taste, and hearing)

HEALTHY SNACKS MOBILE

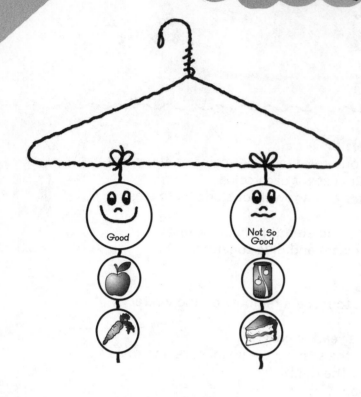

Science Standard
Identifies healthy and
unhealthy food choices

Vocabulary

healthy
Food Guide Pyramid
exercise
nutrients
energy

Discussion

- Because children's stomachs are small, they usually need to eat snacks during the day in order to get all of the essential nutrients their bodies need.
- A good snack is nutrient dense and contributes to the child's intake of healthy foods.
- Children need to become familiar with the Food Guide Pyramid so that they can learn to choose healthy snacks.
- A combination of foods from all five food groups provide children with the fuel their bodies need to grow and with energy to run and play.
- The Food Guide Pyramid includes exercise as part of developing a healthy body.
- Snacks that contain lots of sugar can cause cavities and contribute to children being overweight. These snacks should only be eaten occasionally.

Science Activities
Arts and Crafts Across the Curriculum K, SV 1419023535

Materials

- food pictures on page 92
- one wire hanger per student
- two recycled CD disks per student
- an extra CD for use as a template
- white construction paper
- yarn
- tape
- crayons or markers
- scissors
- glue

Directions

Teacher Preparation

1. Duplicate the food pictures for each student.
2. Tie two CDs to the bottom of the wire hanger with two one-foot pieces of yarn. Loop the yarn through the hole on each CD and tie the ends together over the hanger.
3. Use a small piece of tape to secure the yarn to the hanger to prevent the CDs from sliding.
4. Loop a second piece of yarn that is about two to three feet long through the hole in each CD. Tie the ends together and let this one hang freely.

Student Directions

1. Trace the CD two times on the white construction paper. Cut out both circles.
2. Draw a happy face on one circle and write *Good* below the drawing.
3. Glue it on one of the CDs.
4. Draw a sad face on the second circle and write *Not So Good* below the drawing.
5. Glue it on the other CD.
6. Color and cut out the food pictures.
7. Tape the pictures of healthy snacks to the yarn below the happy face.
8. Tape the pictures of unhealthy snacks to the yarn below the sad face.

Questions

1. What is the Food Guide Pyramid? (It helps people choose foods that are healthy.)
2. How many food groups are on the Food Guide Pyramid? (five)
3. Besides eating good foods, what else does the Food Guide Pyramid suggest people do to stay healthy? (exercise)
4. Name two foods that would be healthy snacks. (Answers will vary.)

Science Activities
Arts and Crafts Across the Curriculum K, SV 1419023535

BATS IN A CAVE

Science Standard
Studies habitat, structure, and behavior of animals

Vocabulary

mammal

fur

wings

nocturnal

pup

Discussion

- Bats are mammals that are covered with fur. They are the only mammal that has wings and can fly.
- They use their wings to catch insects. Their wings are covered with a tough skin and no hair. Their wings have little thumbs on them and are used like hands.
- Bats have live babies called pups that drink milk from the mother's body.
- Bats are nocturnal and sleep upside down. They use the claws on their feet to grasp onto a twig or the interior of cave and hang close together for warmth.
- Bats have teeth and chew their food. Seventy percent of all bats eat insects.

58

Materials

- pattern on page 93
- white construction paper
- brown or gray construction paper
- black ink pad
- soap, water, and towels
- old file folders
- black fine-tip markers
- markers
- scissors
- glue

Directions

Teacher Preparation

1. Cut the brown or gray construction paper in half.
2. Trace and cut out the cave on old file folders for use as a template.

Student Directions

1. Trace the cave template on the brown or gray paper.
2. Cut out the cave.
3. Glue the cave on the white construction paper.
4. Use markers to draw a daytime scene around the cave. Draw the sun, clouds, trees, grass, and flowers.
5. Press one thumb on the black ink pad.
6. Press the thumb and transfer the ink onto the white paper inside the cave to make the body of the bat. Repeat several times.
7. Wash any remaining ink off of the thumb.
8. Turn the picture upside down and draw ears, eyes, nose, mouth and feet on each body with a black marker. The bats will appear to be hanging upside down when the picture is turned.
9. Write or dictate a sentence about the bats such as *Bats sleep during the day.*

Questions

1. Is a bat a bird? (No, it is the only mammal that flies.)
2. What is a mammal covered with? (fur or hair)
3. What do most bats eat? (insects)
4. What does nocturnal mean? (sleep during the day and look for food at night)
5. What are baby bats called and what do they eat? (pups; drink milk from their mother's bodies)
6. Where do some bats go to sleep and stay warm? (in a cave)

PAPER PLATE EARTH

Social Studies Standard
Identifies land masses and large bodies of water on maps and globes

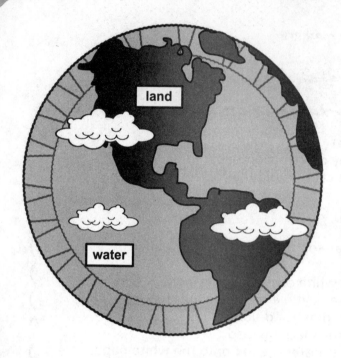

land

water

Vocabulary
Earth
globe
landforms
oceans
continents
atmosphere

Discussion

- Three-fourths of the planet Earth is covered by bodies of water.
- About 97% of the Earth's water is the salt water in the oceans, and only 3% is fresh water.
- Landforms include continents, ocean basins, plains, plateaus, and mountain ranges.
- A globe is a three-dimensional model of the planet Earth that shows where the landforms and bodies of water are.
- The Earth's weather occurs in the atmosphere, which is a layer of air that surrounds the planet.

Social Studies Activities
Arts and Crafts Across the Curriculum K, SV 1419023535

Materials

- one large paper plate per student
- brown and green wax crayons
- blue watercolor paint
- paintbrushes
- cotton balls
- blank index cards
- markers
- scissors
- glue

Directions

Teacher Preparation

1. Draw the outline of the continents as seen on a globe on a paper plate for each student.
2. Cut the index cards into one-by-three-inch pieces for use as labels.

Student Directions

1. Color the continents that indicate land brown and green.
2. Completely cover the rest of the plate with blue watercolor paint for the oceans.
3. Pull apart two or three cotton balls to make them look fluffy like clouds.
4. Glue the cotton balls on the paper plate Earth to indicate clouds.
5. Write the word *land* on a label and glue it on a land area.
6. Write the word *water* on a label and glue it on the ocean or water area.

Questions

1. What is a globe? (a model of the planet Earth)
2. Where is salt water found on Earth? (in the oceans)
3. Is there more salt water or fresh water on Earth? (salt water)
4. Is a continent a body of water or a landform? (landform)
5. What is the atmosphere? (a layer of air that surrounds Earth)

61

MEXICAN BARK PAINTINGS

Social Studies Standard
✳ Identifies customs and traditions

Vocabulary
Mexico
amate paper
bark
design

Discussion

- Mexico is the country directly south of the United States. It borders California, New Mexico, Arizona, and Texas.
- Papermaking is an ancient craft in Mexico.
- Paper called amate is made from the bark of mulberry or fig trees.
- Much of the amate paper is decorated with nature scenes such as birds, trees, animals, and flowers.
- Bright colors are usually used to provide stark contrast on the paper.

Materials

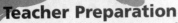

- one brown grocery bag per two students
- black permanent markers
- oil pastels or colored chalk
- tub of water

Directions

Teacher Preparation

1. Tear off the bottom of the grocery bag and tear the seam so that the bag has rough edges and lays flat.
2. Tear each flat section in half.

Student Directions

1. Draw a simple, nature picture on a torn section of the grocery bag with black permanent marker.
2. Draw a decorative border with a permanent black marker around the edge of the section of the grocery bag.
3. Crumple the paper into a ball to give it a bark-like texture.
4. Dip the crumpled paper ball in the tub of water. Squeeze out the excess water.
5. Smooth out and lay the paper flat on a table and allow it to dry.
6. Color each part of the drawing with bright colored chalk or oil pastels. Use a variety of colors.

Questions

1. In what country are bark paintings made? (Mexico)
2. What is bark? (the rough, outside covering of a tree)
3. What is paper made from bark called? (amate)
4. Name the two kinds of trees that are used to make amate. (mulberry and fig)
5. Describe the types of designs found on bark paintings. (nature scenes)

Social Studies Activities
Arts and Crafts Across the Curriculum K, SV 1419023535

LINCOLN PENNY NECKLACE

Social Studies Standard
Identifies the contributions of historical
figures that helped to shape our nation

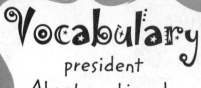

Vocabulary
president
Abraham Lincoln
Civil War
slavery
penny

Discussion

- Abraham Lincoln was the 16th President of the United States.
- He was the president during the Civil War. The war started because some people wanted slaves and others thought it was wrong to have slaves.
- Slavery takes place when a person is owned by and is made to work for another person and does not get paid for the work.
- Lincoln was a great president because he helped to stop slavery.
- Lincoln is honored with his picture on money. He is on the five-dollar bill and on the penny.

Questions

1. Why is the job of the president important? (because the president has to make good choices that help the people and keep them safe)
2. Which president was Abraham Lincoln? (the sixteenth)
3. Why was Lincoln thought to be a great president? (because he helped stop slavery)
4. Which coin is Lincoln's picture on? (the penny)

Materials

- red, white, and blue construction paper
- one Lincoln penny per student
- package of macaroni
- red and blue food coloring
- a milk jug lid, a yogurt container lid, and a coffee can lid
- a teaspoon

- scissors
- gallon size resealable bags
- bottle of rubbing alcohol

- newspapers
- hole punch
- glue
- yarn

Directions

Teacher Preparation

1. Dye half of the package of macaroni red and the other half blue.
2. Place macaroni in the resealable bag. Add a few drops of food coloring and one teaspoon of alcohol.
3. Seal the bag and shake until macaroni is the desired shade of red or blue.
4. Spread the macaroni on newspaper and allow it to dry. Stir it occasionally.
5. Cut a two-foot length of yarn for each student.
6. When students have completed their necklace, tie the ends of the yarn together in a knot.

Student Directions

1. Trace and cut out the lids on construction paper. Cut out a large circle on the blue paper, a medium circle on the white paper, and a small circle on the red paper.
2. Stack the circles from the smallest on top to the largest on bottom.
3. Glue the circles together.
4. Punch two holes in the largest circle.
5. Thread the yarn evenly through the holes.
6. Thread red and blue macaroni in a pattern on each side of the necklace.
7. Have an adult help tie the ends of the yarn together in a knot.
8. Glue the Lincoln penny in the middle of the top circle.

65

Arts and Crafts Across the Curriculum K, SV 1419023535

PAPER BAG WESTERN VEST

Social Studies Standard
Compares life in the past to life in the present

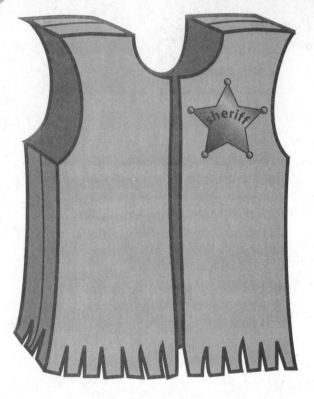

Vocabulary
cowboys
cattle
vests
sheriff
badge

Discussion

- Cowboys developed special clothing that protected them from the harsh conditions associated with working cattle.
- Cowboys wore wide-brimmed hats to protect their faces from the sun.
- The vests they wore helped to keep them warm but also allowed them to move their arms freely when working with cattle or riding horses.
- In the mid-1800s, people in western towns chose a person to enforce the laws. This person was called a marshal, sheriff, or deputy.
- People wore a five- or six-pointed star to identify themselves as law enforcement officers. Today they still wear badges.

Social Studies Activities
Arts and Crafts Across the Curriculum K, SV 1419023535

Materials

- pattern on page 91
- one brown grocery bag per student
- foil
- old file folders
- stapler
- scissors
- glue

Directions

Teacher Preparation

1. Duplicate the star pattern and cut it out.
2. Trace a star shape for each student on file folders.
3. Tear a piece of foil for each student that is big enough to cover the star badge.
4. Cut a bag on the seam from top to bottom.
5. Cut a hole for the neck from the bottom of the bag.
6. Cut two armholes from the sides.
7. Cut across the shoulders so that the bag can lay flat.
8. Turn the bag inside out and staple the shoulders back together. Any advertisement on the bag should now be on the inside of the vest.

Student Directions

1. Use scissors to fringe the bottom edge of the vest.
2. Cut out the star shape for a badge.
3. Cover the badge with foil.
4. Glue the badge to the front of the vest.

Questions

1. What are cattle? (a group of cows)
2. What kind of hat did cowboys wear and why? (hats with wide brims to protect them from the sun)
3. Why did cowboy vests not have sleeves? (so that they could move their arms easily)
4. In the Old West, what was the name of a person who enforced the laws? (a sheriff, marshal, or deputy)
5. What shape is a sheriff's badge? (star shape)

Social Studies Activities
Arts and Crafts Across the Curriculum K, SV 1419023535

STARS AND STRIPES FLAG

Social Studies Standard
Identifies the flag
as a national symbol

Vocabulary

symbol
United States
flag
stars
stripes

Discussion

- A national flag is a piece of cloth that is flown to identify a country.
- Each country determines the symbols and colors that make up the design of its flag.
- The United States flag has 13 stripes that represent the original 13 colonies. Seven stripes are red and 6 are white.
- It also has 50 white stars on a blue background that represent the 50 states.
- The United States flag has undergone several changes since the first one in 1877. A star was added each time a state joined the union.

Social Studies Activities
Arts and Crafts Across the Curriculum K, SV 1419023535

Materials

- plastic wrap with bubbles
- white construction paper
- old cookie sheet
- red and blue paint
- silver foil star stickers
- paintbrushes
- masking tape
- markers
- scissors

Directions

Teacher Preparation

1. Use a black marker to draw the blue field and thirteen stripes of the United States flag on a piece of white construction paper.
2. Tape the outline of the flag to the cookie sheet.
3. Cut a piece of plastic wrap that is slightly larger than the size of the construction paper.
4. Tape the plastic wrap on top of the flag outline.
5. Use masking tape to cover six sections of the plastic wrap that would be the white stripes on the United States flag.

Student Directions

1. Paint the upper left-hand corner of the plastic wrap blue.
2. Paint red stripes on the plastic wrap.
3. Lay a piece of white paper on the painted plastic wrap.
4. Gently rub the paper with flattened hands.
5. Lift the paper off of the plastic wrap and allow the paint to dry.
6. Arrange 50 star stickers in rows to resemble the flag.

Questions

1. What is a national flag? (a piece of cloth that identifies a country)
2. How many stripes are there on the United States flag? (thirteen)
3. What color are the stripes on the flag? How many are there of each color? (7 red and 6 white)
4. How many stars are currently on the United States flag? (fifty)
5. How does the design change on the United States flag when a new state joins the union? (Another star is added.)

Social Studies Activities
Arts and Crafts Across the Curriculum K, SV 1419023535

FAST FIRETRUCK

My firetruck is red.

Vocabulary
firefighter
tanker truck
pumper truck
ladder truck
turnouts

Discussion

- Firefighters are responsible for protecting people's lives and property and the environment.
- When they are fighting a fire, firefighters must wear protective clothing and an air tank.
- The pants that firefighters wear are called "turnouts" because they are turned inside out with boots attached when they are not being used.
- A pumper truck carries some water and is usually sent to the scene of accidents.
- The tanker truck holds more than 1,000 gallons of water and is sent if more water is needed.
- The ladder truck is much longer and has a 100-foot ladder with a bucket for reaching fires higher up.

Questions

1. How does a firefighter help the community? (puts out fires and rescues people)
2. What are turnouts? (the pants that firefighters wear)
3. Which truck is usually sent to the scene of an accident? (pumper truck)
4. What is the truck called that carries a 100-foot ladder? (ladder truck)

Social Studies Activities
Arts and Crafts Across the Curriculum K, SV 1419023535

Materials

- pattern on page 94
- light blue, red, and black construction paper
- baby food jar lids
- craft sticks
- black pipe cleaners
- brads
- red glitter
- glue
- old file folders
- markers
- scissors

- masking tape

Directions

Teacher Preparation

1. Trace and cut out the firetruck on file folders to use as a template.
2. Help students attach the wheels to the firetruck using the brads.
3. Cover the tip of the pipe cleaners with masking tape for the fire hose. Provide one for each student.
4. Help students attach the pipe cleaner to the paper by poking one end through and taping it on the back of the paper.

Student Directions

1. Trace and cut out the firetruck template on red construction paper.
2. Cut out the window. Younger students may need help.
3. Glue the firetruck on the light blue construction paper.
4. Trace and cut out two circles on black construction paper using the jar lid as a template.
5. Have an adult help poke a brad through the center of each wheel and attach the wheels to the truck. Press the brads open on the back side of the paper.
6. Squeeze a small amount of glue on the top of the truck. Sprinkle it with red glitter for the siren light.
7. Glue two craft sticks parallel to each other on the side of the truck for the ladder. Use a marker to draw the rungs of the ladder.
8. Wrap the pipe cleaner around a marker to give it the look of a coiled water hose.
9. Have an adult help poke the end of the pipe cleaner through the construction paper and tape it in place on the back. Position the hose next to the ladder.
10. Write or dictate a sentence about the firetruck such as *My firetruck is red.*

Social Studies Activities
Arts and Crafts Across the Curriculum K, SV 1419023535

BIG RED BARN AND SILO

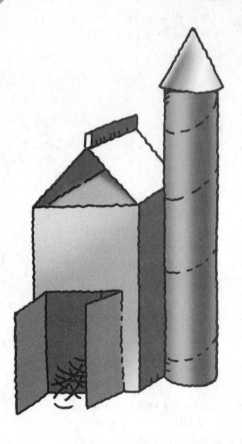

Social Studies Standard
Understands how basic human needs of food can be met

Vocabulary
farm
barn
silo
crops
animals

Discussion

- Farms provide the sources for many products, especially food, that are used or consumed by people.
- The average farmer grows enough food to feed about 129 people.
- Crops are plants grown for human or animal consumption or use.
- Barns are used for storage of farm machinery, tools, seeds, or hay. Barns are also used as shelter for animals.
- Animal feed is stored in silos that are attached to barns.
- Many animals are raised on a farm to provide food. For example, beef and milk come from cows, and poultry and eggs come from chickens.

Social Studies Activities
Arts and Crafts Across the Curriculum K, SV 1419023535

Materials

- one clean, half-gallon milk or juice carton per student
- one paper towel tube per student
- one cone cup per student
- red and gray tempera paint
- retractable utility knife
- hay (or yellow basket grass)
- paintbrushes

- hot glue gun
- glue

Directions

Teacher Preparation
1. Use the knife to cut a door in the bottom of the carton.
2. Use hot glue to attach the tube to the carton to look like a barn and silo.

Student Directions
1. Paint the sides of the carton and the tube red to resemble a barn and silo.
2. Paint the top of the carton and the cone cup gray.
3. Glue the cone on top of the tube for the silo.
4. Glue hay on the barn floor.

Questions

1. Why are farms important? (Much of the food people eat or use is grown on a farm.)
2. What is a crop? (plants grown for people or animals to eat or use)
3. What might be found in a barn? (Answers will vary.)
4. What are silos used for? (to store animal feed)
5. List animals that might live on a farm. (Answers will vary.)

Social Studies Activities
Arts and Crafts Across the Curriculum K, SV 1419023535

FAMILY QUILT

Vocabulary

family
father
mother
brother
sister
sibling

Discussion

- A family is a group of people who are usually related and who live together.
- The immediate family can be a group of two or more people.
- There needs to be at least one adult to care for any children in the family.
- The extended family is a group of related people like grandparents, cousins, aunts, and uncles who live in different places.
- A person can have many names in a family such as mother, sister, grandmother, and daughter.
- *Sibling* is another name for a brother or sister.

Social Studies Activities
Arts and Crafts Across the Curriculum K, SV 1419023535

Materials

- large construction paper— various colors
- white construction paper
- tape
- markers or crayons
- scissors
- glue

Directions

 Teacher Preparation

1. Cut six three-inch squares from white construction paper for each student.
2. Tape together two pieces of construction paper for students who have families with more than six members and provide them with the correct number of white squares.
3. Have students decorate extra squares if their family has fewer than six members.

Student Directions

1. Draw a picture of each member of your family on a square paper.
2. Write or dictate each person's name below their picture.
3. Glue at least six squares on a large piece of construction paper to resemble a quilt. Use a larger piece of construction paper for bigger families.
4. On one blank square, write or dictate the name of your family, such as *The Jones Family.*
5. Use markers or crayons to decorate any remaining blank squares.

Questions

1. How many people are in your family? (Answers will vary.)
2. Do all people have brothers and sisters? (No, some have only a sister, some have only a brother, some have both, and some have none.)
3. Who are the grandparents in a family? (the father and mother of the parents)
4. How many people are in an immediate family? (two or more)
5. What is a sibling? (a brother or a sister)

75

KWANZAA CANDLES

Social Studies Standard
Compares family
customs and traditions

Vocabulary

Kwanzaa
African-American
kinara
mishumaa saba
candles

Discussion

- Kwanzaa is a nonreligious holiday that was created in 1966 by Dr. Maulana Karenga as a way to reinforce community, family, and culture.
- Kwanzaa lasts for seven days beginning on December 26 and ending on January 1.
- A candle holder called a kinara represents African-American ancestors.
- The kinara holds seven candles with one black, three red, and three green candles. The candles are called the mishumaa saba.
- The black candle is in the middle and is lit on the first day of Kwanzaa.

Arts and Crafts Across the Curriculum K, SV 1419023535

Materials

- seven bathroom tissue rolls per student
- yellow tissue paper
- red, green, and black tempera paint
- paintbrushes
- paper clips
- scissors
- glue

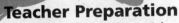

Directions

Teacher Preparation
Cut tissue paper into 4-inch squares. Provide each student with 7 squares.

Student Directions
1. Paint 3 tissue rolls red. Allow them to dry.
2. Paint 3 tissue rolls green. Allow them to dry.
3. Paint 1 tissue roll black. Allow it to dry.
4. Squeeze a line of glue on the sides of the red tissue rolls.
5. Stand the tissue rolls side by side so that the glue will hold the rolls together. Place a paper clip over the top edges of the rolls to hold them in place while the glue dries.
6. Repeat steps 4 and 5 with the green tissue rolls.
7. Repeat steps 4 and 5 to glue the red tissue rolls to the left of the black roll and the green rolls to the right of the black roll.
8. Gently crumple a piece of yellow tissue paper for each tissue roll and place it in the end of the roll for the candle flame.

Questions
1. What African-American holiday was created in 1966? (Kwanzaa)
2. During which month does the celebration of Kwanzaa begin? (December)
3. What is a kinara? (a candle holder)
4. How many candles does a kinara hold? (seven)
5. Name the colors of the seven candles for Kwanzaa. (one black, three red, three green)
6. Tell how your family uses candles to celebrate a special day or holiday. (Answers will vary.)

Social Studies Activities
Arts and Crafts Across the Curriculum K, SV 1419023535

JULY FOURTH HEADBAND

Social Studies Standard
Identifies customs associated with national patriotic holidays

Vocabulary
Independence Day
Fourth of July
holiday
parade
fireworks

Discussion

- Independence Day is also known as the Fourth of July and the birthday of the United States of America.
- The Fourth of July is a holiday or a day off from work for people to celebrate the adoption of the *Declaration of Independence* on July 4, 1776.
- The Fourth of July was set aside as a national holiday in 1941.
- The day was originally celebrated in 1776 with a parade and cannon fire. The tradition of parades on Independence Day is continued throughout today.
- Fireworks take the place of cannon fire today.

Social Studies Activities
Arts and Crafts Across the Curriculum K, SV 1419023535

Materials

- pattern on page 91
- one sentence strip per student
- red, white, and blue crepe paper streamers
- white construction paper
- silver glitter
- scissors
- glue
- stapler

Directions

Teacher Preparation

1. Duplicate stars on white construction paper. Provide three stars per student.
2. Mark the center of the sentence strips with an *X* to indicate where to glue the center star.
3. Cut several 18-inch streamers for each student.
4. After students have added the stars on the sentence strip, measure and staple the ends to make a headband.

Student Directions

1. Cut out three stars.
2. Spread a thin layer of glue on the stars and cover them with glitter.
3. Glue the stars on the sentence strip with the middle one on the *X*.
4. Have an adult measure the sentence strip and staple the ends together to make a headband.
5. Glue the ends of several crepe paper strips to the back of the headband so that they hang freely.

Questions

1. Why do we celebrate Independence Day? (It is the birthday of the United States.)
2. On what date is the holiday to celebrate Independence Day? (July 4th)
3. What was different about Independence Day when it was made a national holiday? (People got a day off from work to celebrate.)
4. Describe what might be seen in a Fourth of July parade. (Answers will vary.)
5. What is used today to celebrate Independence Day instead of cannon fire? (fireworks)

79

PILGRIM CENTERPIECES

Social Studies Standard
Identifies family customs and traditions and explains their importance

Vocabulary
Pilgrims
Mayflower
Squanto
harvest
Thanksgiving

Discussion

- The Pilgrims sailed from England on the *Mayflower* on September 16, 1620, in search of religious freedom.
- In the spring of 1621, the Pilgrims met Squanto who was a member of the Wamponoag tribe.
- He showed them how to hunt and fish and how best to plant seeds.
- There were many crops gathered and the harvest was bountiful.
- Sometime in mid-October, the Pilgrims invited Chief Massasoit and the Wamponoag tribe to celebrate the bountiful harvest. They celebrated for three days.
- In 1863, Thanksgiving was declared a national holiday by President Abraham Lincoln on the last day in November. It was moved to the third Thursday in November in 1939.

Materials

- patterns on page 95
- brown or white lunch sacks
- black, white, and pink construction paper
- 2" yellow paper squares
- newspapers
- plastic coffee can lids
- old file folders
- stapler
- markers
- scissors
- glue

Directions

Teacher Preparation

1. Duplicate and cut out the hats and collar patterns.
2. Trace them on the file folders for use as a template. Cut them out.
3. Trace the boy's hat on black paper. Provide one for each boy.
4. Trace the girl's hat on white paper. Provide one for each girl.
5. Trace a collar on white paper for each student.
6. Help students staple the sack closed when they have stuffed it with newspaper.

Student Directions

1. Stuff the lunch sack with newspaper.
2. Have an adult help staple the sack closed.
3. Trace a coffee can lid on pink paper and cut it out for the face.
4. Draw eyes, nose, mouth, and hair on the circle with markers.
5. Glue the face on the side of the sack.
6. Cut out the hat and collar.
7. Glue it on the sack to complete the Pilgrim face.
8. Glue a small square of yellow paper for the buckle on the boy's hat.

Questions

1. What was the name of the ship that the Pilgrim's sailed on to America? (*Mayflower*)
2. What did Squanto teach them to do? (hunt, fish, and plant seeds)
3. How did the Pilgrims say thank you to Squanto and his tribe for helping them? (invited them to a celebration)
4. What do people do today to celebrate Thanksgiving? (get together with family, eat dinner, watch parades or football games)
5. Tell about something that you are thankful for. (Answers will vary.)

Social Studies Activities
Arts and Crafts Across the Curriculum K, SV 1419023535

SHOE BOX STORES

Vocabulary

barter
trade
stores
coins
malls

Discussion

- Long ago people bartered, or traded, to get the goods they needed. They bartered animals, produce, leather, and even sugar.
- Coins came into use when bartering became too complicated of a way to obtain the goods and services that were needed.
- People have jobs to earn money to pay for goods and services.
- Specialty stores have merchandise related to a certain area such as a pet store, clothing store, or food store.
- Malls are large shopping complexes that house stores, businesses, and restaurants that are easily accessible to pedestrians.

Materials

- one shoe box per student
- craft paper
- construction paper
- magazines
- tape
- markers
- scissors
- glue

Directions

Teacher Preparation

1. Cover the top and bottom of a shoe box with craft paper.
2. Cut different colors of construction paper into small rectangles and squares for windows, doors, and signs.

Student Directions

1. Choose a kind of store.
2. Glue construction paper windows and a door on the outside of the box lid.
3. Draw or cut out pictures from magazines of things that the store would sell to "display" in the windows.
4. Write the name of the store on a card to make a sign.
5. Glue the sign on the outside of the box lid.
6. Cut out pictures of things to sell in the store.
7. Glue the pictures inside the box.

Questions

1. What does bartering mean? (to trade things)
2. What did people start to use when bartering was too complicated? (coins)
3. What kind of store would sell kittens? (a pet store)
4. Why do people have jobs? (to earn money to buy things they need)
5. Name some stores or businesses that might be found in a mall. (Answers will vary.)

83

LETTER PATTERNS

Use with "Alphabet Blocks" on page 8.

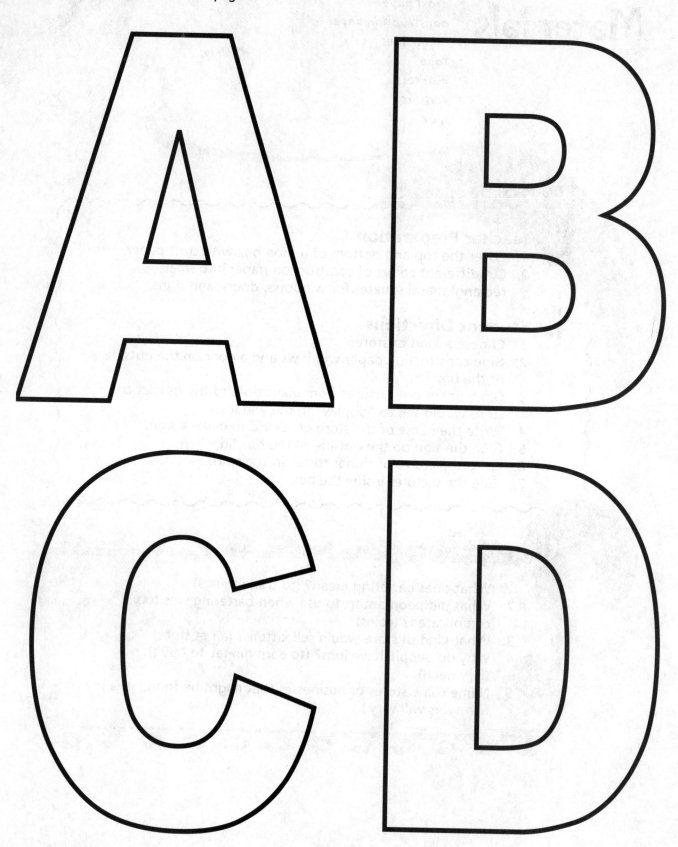

Patterns
Arts and Crafts Across the Curriculum K, SV 1419023535

PAPER PLATE MASK PATTERNS

Use with "Little Red Hen Story Masks" on page 14, "Little Pig Sack Puppet" on page 18, and "Tissue Box Piggy Bank" on page 24.

85

Patterns
Arts and Crafts Across the Curriculum K, SV 1419023535

FISH PATTERNS

Use with "Opposites in a Fishbowl" on page 10.

SQUIRREL PATTERNS

Use with "Squirrel in a Tree" on page 26.

Patterns
Arts and Crafts Across the Curriculum K, SV 1419023535

CLOCK AND MOUSE PATTERNS

Use with "Hickory Dickory Box Clock" on page 30.

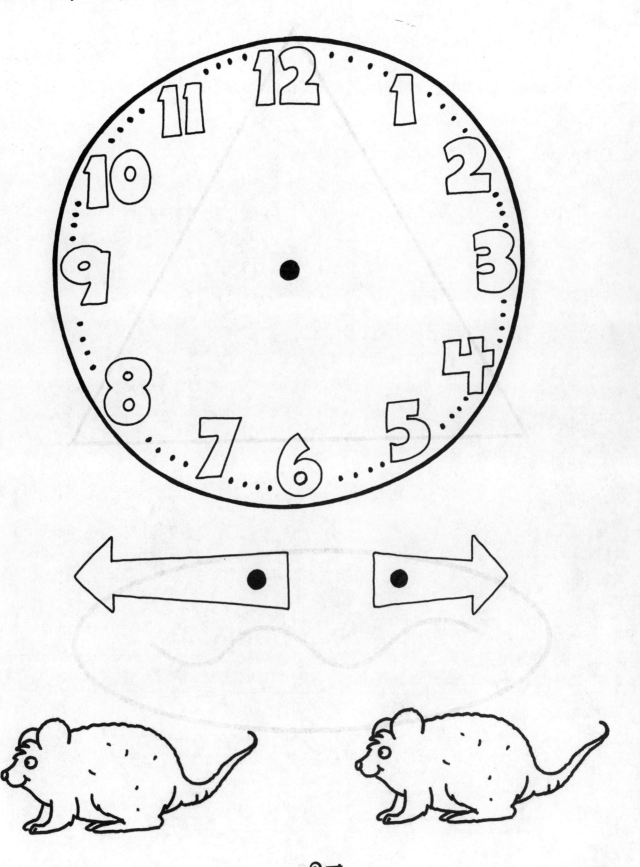

Patterns
Arts and Crafts Across the Curriculum K, SV 1419023535

HAT AND MOUTH PATTERNS

Use with "Shapely Clown" on page 34.

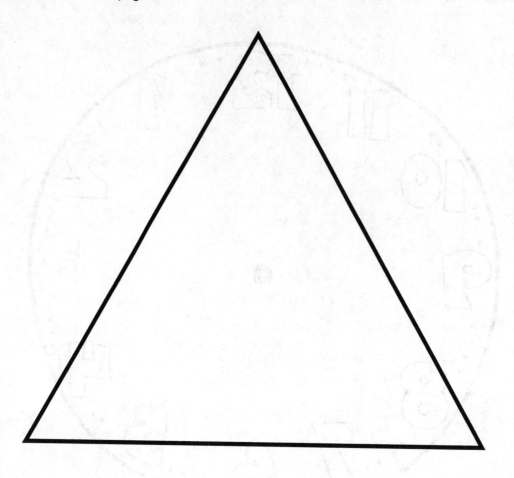

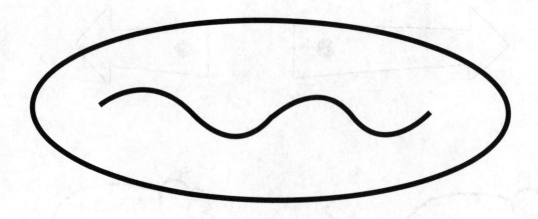

Arts and Crafts Across the Curriculum K, SV 1419023535

BUTTERFLY PATTERNS

Use with "Windsock Butterfly" on page 44.

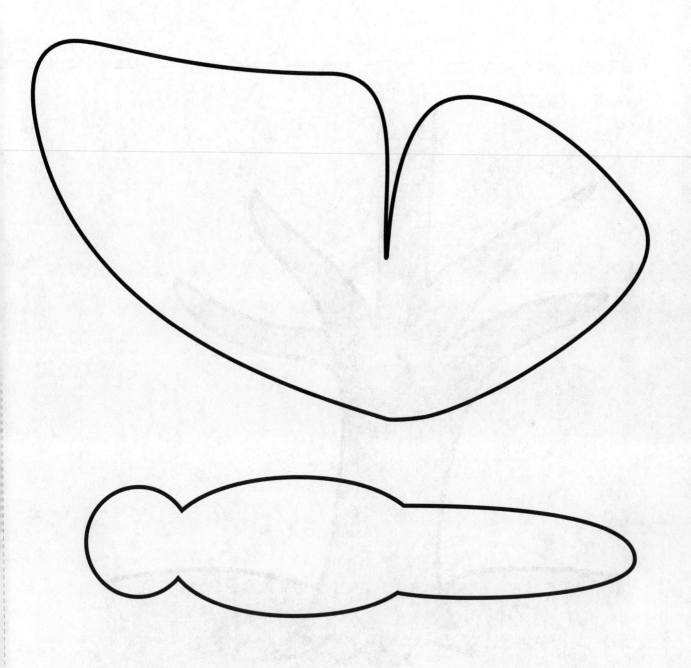

Patterns
Arts and Crafts Across the Curriculum K, SV 1419023535

TREE PATTERN

Use with "Seasonal Tissue Box" on page 50.

Patterns
Arts and Crafts Across the Curriculum K, SV 1419023535

TURTLE PATTERN

Use with "Turtle Magnet" on page 52.

STAR PATTERN

Use with "Paper Bag Western Vest" on page 66 and with "July Fourth Headband" on page 78.

FOOD PICTURES

Use with "Healthy Snacks Mobile" on page 56.

Patterns
Arts and Crafts Across the Curriculum K, SV 1419023535

BAT CAVE PATTERN

Use with "Bats in a Cave" on page 58.

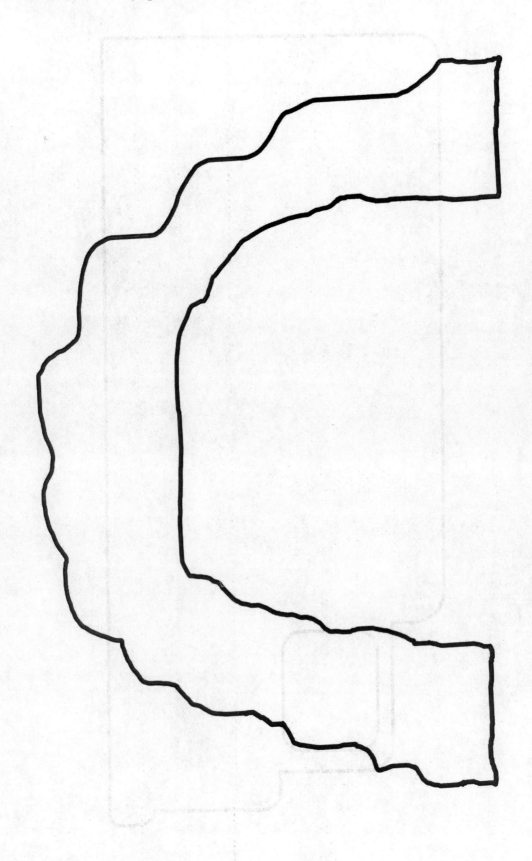

Patterns
Arts and Crafts Across the Curriculum K, SV 1419023535

FIRETRUCK PATTERN

Use with "Fast Firetruck" on page 70.

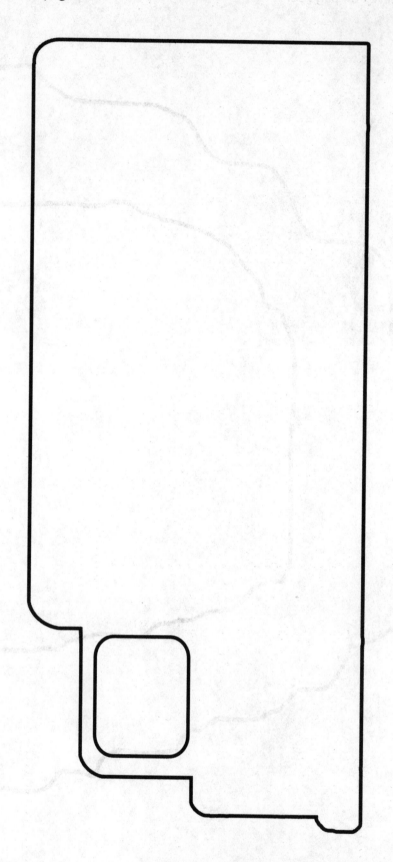

Patterns
Arts and Crafts Across the Curriculum K, SV 1419023535

PILGRIM PATTERNS

Use with "Pilgrim Centerpieces" on page 80.

95

Patterns
Arts and Crafts Across the Curriculum K, SV 1419023535

ALPHABETICAL INDEX

Index
Arts and Crafts Across the Curriculum K, SV 1419023535